Geographic Features

Elise Wallace

Consultant

Crystal Hahm, M.A., Ed.M.
Tustin Unified School District

Bijan Kazerooni, M.A.
Chapman University

Publishing Credits

Rachelle Cracchiolo, M.S.Ed., *Publisher*
Conni Medina, M.A.Ed., *Managing Editor*
Emily R. Smith, M.A.Ed., *Series Developer*
June Kikuchi, *Content Director*
Susan Daddis, M.A.Ed., *Editor*
Courtney Roberson, *Senior Graphic Designer*

Image Credits: p.23 B.A.E. Inc./Alamy; p.24 Granger Academic; all other images from iStock and/or Shutterstock.

Library of Congress Cataloging-in-Publication Data

Names: Wallace, Elise, author.
Title: Geographic features / Elise Wallace.
Description: Huntington Beach, CA : Teacher Created Materials, Inc., 2018. | Includes index. | Audience: K to Grade 3.
Identifiers: LCCN 2017053305 (print) | LCCN 2018006116 (ebook) | ISBN 9781425825614 | ISBN 9781425825195 (pbk.)
Subjects: LCSH: United States--Geography--Juvenile literature.
Classification: LCC E161.3 (ebook) | LCC E161.3 .W35 2018 (print) | DDC 917.3--dc23
LC record available at https://lccn.loc.gov/2017053305

Teacher Created Materials

5301 Oceanus Drive
Huntington Beach, CA 92649-1030
www.tcmpub.com

ISBN 978-1-4258-2519-5

© 2018 Teacher Created Materials, Inc.
Printed by: 926. Printed In: Malaysia. PO#: PO9231

Table of Contents

What Is Geography?

The United States has it all. There are beaches and mountains. There are forests and deserts. It is a very **diverse** land.

There are many ways to look at the country's land. First, it can be explored by its physical geography, or the land's natural features. These include landforms, climate, wildlife, and **resources**.

The second way is through human geography. This is the study of how humans connect with the land. It includes how we **adapt** and change the land. We will use these two ways to explore the country's **regions**. The regions are coasts, mountains, plains, and deserts.

Ocean Views

One of the best ways to explore the West Coast is to drive on U.S. Route 101. This road runs along the coast. It is over 1,500 miles (2,414 kilometers) of breathtaking views!

The United States is part of North America.

Landforms and Climate

The physical geography of the United States has many features. The country is bordered on the east and west by oceans. These are huge bodies of salt water. They cover most of the world. There are also smaller bodies of water in the country. One example is lakes. Lakes are surrounded by land.

Two land features in the United States are mountains and hills. Mountains are landforms that tower over the surrounding land. Hills are also landforms. They are like mountains but not as high.

Across the country, you can also find plains and deserts. Plains are large areas of land with few trees. They are found between mountains and hills. Deserts are large areas that are lower than the surrounding land. They are dry. Not much grows there.

The Great Lakes

The five Great Lakes are on the border the United States shares with Canada. They provide one-fifth of the world's fresh water. The five lakes combined are larger than the state of Texas!

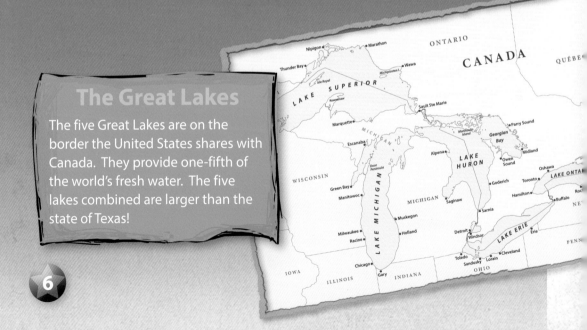

ocean

lake

mountains

hills

plains

desert

Anchorage, Alaska, is on the coast. This makes it easy to ship oil from there.

Climate is a type of physical feature. It is the **typical** weather of a place over a long time. Natural resources are also a physical feature. They are things such as clean water and good soil. These things are used for farming. They make it easier for people to live in an area. People also sell resources, such as oil and salt.

Climate and resources affect where people live. Some people choose to live in places where the weather is not too hot or too cold. They move to places that have access to the resources they need.

Extreme Cold

How cold does it get in your state? Almost every state has logged nights when the temperature dipped below zero. Only one state hasn't. It is Hawai'i. The coldest temperature there was 12°F (-11°C).

Coast to Coast

Water surrounds most of the United States. Oceans border almost two-thirds of the country. Along the East Coast is the Atlantic Ocean. It was the first ocean to be crossed by ship and by plane. Along the West Coast is the Pacific Ocean. It is the largest ocean in the world. The Ring of Fire is located here. It has most of the world's active volcanoes.

Both oceans supply the country with resources. These include oil and natural gas. Fishing is a key **industry**. Cod and lobster are caught in the Atlantic. Salmon and tuna are caught in the Pacific. The oceans help trade, too. Huge ships travel to and from the **ports** on both coasts. These ships deliver goods to other countries.

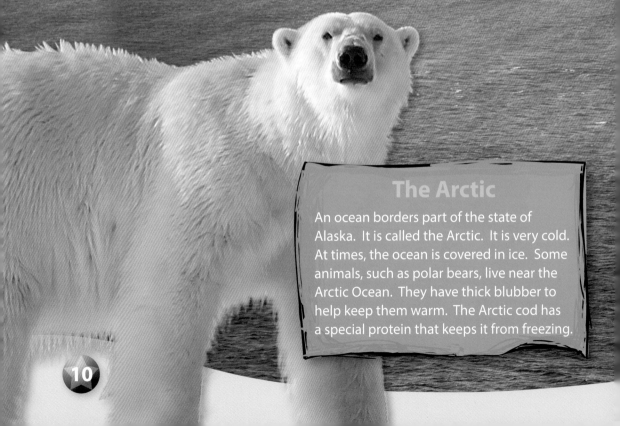

The Arctic

An ocean borders part of the state of Alaska. It is called the Arctic. It is very cold. At times, the ocean is covered in ice. Some animals, such as polar bears, live near the Arctic Ocean. They have thick blubber to help keep them warm. The Arctic cod has a special protein that keeps it from freezing.

Oceans border much of the United States.

A ship moves goods to ports around the world.

Living on the Coast

The Atlantic coast was the first part of the country to be explored by people from Europe. The first settlers came in the 1600s. They came to start new lives. They wanted to be able to practice their religion freely. As more and more people moved there, the coast became crowded. Cities grew larger. Some people moved farther **inland**.

Fountain of Youth

Florida's Atlantic coast is home to the oldest city in the country. It is St. Augustine. In 1513, an explorer landed there. He was searching for the Fountain of Youth. Today, people can visit the spring he found. Visitors can try their luck and drink the water!

Spanish settlers came to the Pacific coast in the 1700s. After the Spanish claimed the land, they mapped out the coast. The land's early **culture** grew out of churches called missions. Towns and farms were built around these places.

Today, most people in the United States live near the coasts. They are drawn by the mild climates. They move for work, too. There are many jobs at ports on both coasts. Tourists from all over the world come to enjoy the beaches.

Mission San Luis Rey was called King of the Missions because of its size and amount of land.

The Mountains

Mountains make up a large part of the United States. They are home to many kinds of plants and creatures.

The Appalachian Mountains are about 2,000 miles (3,200 kilometers) long. This range has the longest marked hiking trail in the country. The trail goes from Georgia to Maine!

The Rocky Mountains are found between the Great Plains and the West Coast. This range goes through six states and into Canada. It is 3,000 mi. (4,800 km) long. Pikes Peak is found in this range. It is the second-most visited peak in the world!

The Sierra Nevada are in California. This range is over 250 mi. (400 km) long. Its tallest mountain is Mount Whitney. That is the most climbed peak in this range.

All three ranges are home to several national parks. Millions of people visit them each year.

Mt. Whitney

The Home of Big Foot

Ever heard of the legend of Big Foot? For hundreds of years, people have spoken of a tall, hairy beast. It is said to lurk in the forests of the Colorado Rockies. Some describe him as 10 feet (3 meters) tall!

BIG FOOT XING

Living in the Mountains

After settling on the coasts, people began moving inland. To get there, they sometimes had to cross mountain ranges. In the 1800s, people began moving east to west for more land. They stopped in mountain passes. **Trading posts** were built along the trails. Towns and cities grew from these trading posts.

Yellowstone National Park has had more than one million visitors every year since 1948.

Today, many people visit the mountains. They like to spend time in the great outdoors. They want to see the trees, plants, and wildlife found there. The country's mountain regions have large parks. Tourists come from all over the world. They want to spend time at forest resorts. The government protects much of the land in the parks.

Still, tourism has taken its toll on some of these places. Lakes and streams have become polluted. Campfires and cars pollute the air. The noise people and cars make can scare wildlife.

Protect the Parks

Yellowstone National Park asks visitors to take the Yellowstone Pledge. It says that people should not do any harm to the parks. It tells them to travel safely and respect wildlife. Guests pledge to dispose of trash properly and to find a ranger if someone is doing something dangerous in the park.

The Great Plains

The Great Plains region is a large **plateau**. It is known for its grasslands. Some parts are very flat and covered by **prairies**. There are also low hills and valleys. There are even tree-covered mountains, such as the Black Hills of South Dakota. Parts of ten states make up the Great Plains.

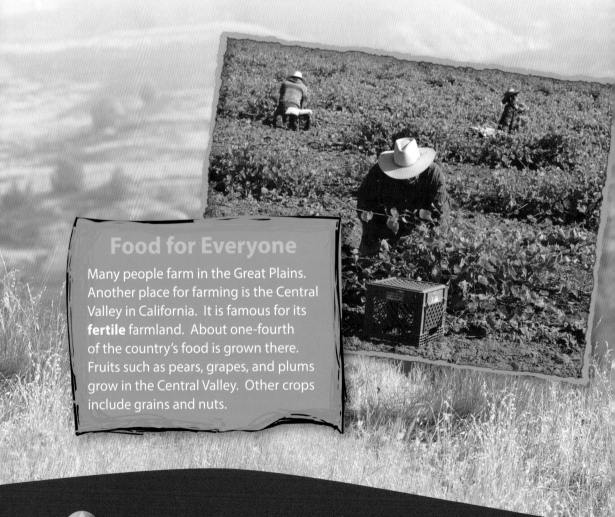

Food for Everyone

Many people farm in the Great Plains. Another place for farming is the Central Valley in California. It is famous for its **fertile** farmland. About one-fourth of the country's food is grown there. Fruits such as pears, grapes, and plums grow in the Central Valley. Other crops include grains and nuts.

Rivers run through the Great Plains. The two most important ones are the Mississippi and Missouri rivers. They are used to move people, goods, and water to other parts of the country.

The climate of the Great Plains can be extreme. The summers can be scorching hot, and the winters can be freezing cold.

Bison have lived on the Great Plains for thousands of years.

Living on the Great Plains

Many years before people from Europe settled on the Great Plains, it was home to large herds of bison. American Indians hunted the bison. No part went to waste. The hides were used to make clothing or to cover homes. Meat was dried and eaten. Even the hair and hooves were used.

In the late 1800s, settlers and ranchers forced the American Indian tribes to adapt to their way of life or move off the land. Cattle replaced the bison. Wheat farmers began to crowd the cattle ranchers. In the 1930s, a **drought** made it hard to grow crops. Many farmers left to find work in other places.

Today, the Great Plains region is used mostly for farming. Wheat, cotton, corn, and hay are grown there. Cattle and sheep are raised there, too.

Going Batty

Austin, the capital of Texas, is in the Great Plains. It has the most bats of any urban area in the country. More than one million bats **migrate** in the spring to live under a bridge in the city. Visitors come at dusk to watch the bats as they leave to find food.

The Deserts

The two largest deserts in the United States are in the western half of the country. The Great Basin Desert is the largest. It is between the Rocky Mountains and the Sierra Nevada. The climate there is quite cold, unlike most deserts. Snowfall is common.

This desert is home to many animals. These include mountain lions, coyotes, and bighorn sheep. Bristlecone pine trees are found here. They are the oldest living things in the world.

One of the most well-known deserts is the Mojave. It is in California, Arizona, and Nevada. The climate here can change from day to day. On some days, the heat is brutal. On others, the weather is cool.

The Mojave is home to lizards, bats, foxes, and other creatures. Plants are sparse in this region. Only a few plants, such as cacti, grow there. All desert life must be able to adapt to the changing climate.

Chihuahuan Desert

The United States shares a desert with Mexico. It is the Chihuahuan Desert. Carlsbad Caverns National Park is located here. There aren't any rivers or streams in the park. But, there are over 119 caves to explore. A main attraction is the Big Room. It's bigger than six football fields!

Living in the Desert

American Indians were the first people to live in the deserts. The Mojave Desert is named after a native tribe. The Mojave people lived in the Southwest. They lived off the land. They used the Colorado River as a water source for farming. When the river flooded, it watered their crops.

The Mojave people hunted and fished.

Today, most of the Mojave is undeveloped. This means that not many people live in the region. The climate is too hot for most people. The desert is used as a natural resource. In 2013, a large solar farm was built in the Mojave. This farm harvests sunlight. The sunlight is used to power homes. There are also wind farms in the desert. Some of these wind farms are the largest in the country.

A Diverse Land

The United States is big and stunning. Its physical geography has many features. The country has oceans, mountains, plains, and deserts. It has many resources. People have used and adapted these resources to survive.

Splashy Sight

Yosemite National Park is in California. Many people come to the park to see its waterfalls. They are some of the world's tallest falls. They are created by snow that has melted.

Think about where you live. What is the climate like? Is it warm or cold? Do you know the resources found in your town? Think about the landforms and bodies of water. Do you have mountains and lakes?

Every place has its own features and resources. That is what makes each place unique. People settle in places for many reasons. The first people who settled in your town thought about climate and resources. They stayed because the land allowed them to **thrive**!

Sing It!

Pick your favorite region that you read about in this book. Do some research on it. Then, write a rap or song about its natural wonders. Sing your rap or song to your friends and family.

America the Beautiful.

KATHARINE LEE BATES.
By permission.

WILLIAM L. GLOVER.

1 O beau - ti - ful for spa - cious skies, For am - ber waves of grain, For pur - ple moun-tain maj - es-ties, A - bove the fruit - ed plain. A - mer - i - ca! A - mer - i - ca! God shed His grace on thee, And crown thy good with brotherhood From sea to shin -ing sea!

Glossary

adapt—to change something so it serves a different or better purpose

culture—the beliefs and ways of a group of people

diverse—made up of things that are different from each other

drought—a long time without rain

fertile—capable of supporting the growth of many plants

industry—group of businesses that provide specific products or services

inland—away from a coast

migrate—to move from one place to another at a certain time of year

plateau—a big area of land higher than the land around it

ports—cities where ships bring goods and people

prairies—large, flat lands covered mostly with grasses

regions—parts of a country that are different from other parts

resources—things that a country has and can use to make money

thrive—to have great success

trading posts—stores set up in areas with few people to trade

typical—usual or normal for that area

Index

Your Turn!

Find your home state on the map above. What land forms and bodies of water are nearby? What is the climate? Write a poem about how geography affects where you live.